CRYSTAL JEWELLERY

Project Book

Learn how to create a collection of Jewellery

5 projects inside

INTRODUCTION

Welcome to the wonderful world of Crystal Jewellery!

This kit has been specifically designed for adults only.

Learning a new skill is always exciting – we're here to help you get started. Wire wrapping is one of the most simplistic, elegant ways to make jewellery with next to no tools or expenditure. All you need is some easy to bend wire and whatever object you'd like to wire wrap!

Anyone can learn to wire wrap. It's one of the most popular and low maintenance techniques in jewellery making, as you can wrap almost anything in wire. This could be a crystal, a stone, a bead, or even a piece of ceramic (you will see this a little bit later).

As well as making yourself some interesting and unique designs, you can also use your wire to create loops and hooks to join other components to your centre piece. By creating a loop with your wire, you can then decide whether to attach a necklace chain or even a pair of earring hooks to your pieces to make them wearable and more versatile.

The best thing about wire wrapping crystals, is that no two pieces will ever be the same. Yes, you can follow the same technique with your wire, but because of the nature of your crystal - the outcome of your pieces will always be different. And don't forget, if you start to wrap your wire around your crystal following a specific technique, you can always change direction if you want to go a different way. There is no right or wrong way to wrap your wire. As long as your centre piece is secured in place amongst your wire, then you have successfully wire wrapped yourself a piece of jewellery!

This kit provides everything you need to make your first piece of art, which means getting started is easy. We have also included four other projects within this book to help you along the way. Just like any new craft, wire wrapping can be a little tricky at first. Be patient and take your time, but most importantly, enjoy yourself.

WHAT'S INCLUDED:

- 1x Large crystal for necklace
- 2x Smaller crystals for earrings
- Gold coloured wire
- 1x Gold coloured chain with clasps
- 1x Pair of earring hooks

WHAT YOU'LL NEED:

- Round nose pliers
- Flat nose pliers
- Pencil
- Wire cutters

WRAPPING TECHNIQUES

There really is no right or wrong way to wire wrap crystals, but two techniques which we guarantee you will use in almost any wire wrap would be:

TWISTING WIRE

The easiest way to twist your wire is to get a really firm grasp with a pair of round nose pliers. Hold your pliers in one hand and your wire in the other and twist as tightly as you can. This can then be used to create a hook, or as decoration on a piece you have already made.

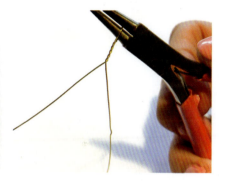

CROSSING OVER

Both pictures below are examples of crossing over your wire. You can cross this in a symmetrical way, or you can completely go off grid and cross over side to side and horizontally. You can either use one piece of wire as shown in the right picture, or use two pieces held together as shown in the left.

CRYSTAL JEWELLERY THE BASICS:

To start your wire wrapping journey, all you will need is your chosen wire and the object that you would like to wrap. A pencil and wire cutters will also be useful. In this make, we are using one larger crystal piece to create a pendant, and two smaller pieces to create drop down earrings.

PICKING YOUR WIRE:

It really doesn't matter what colour wire you choose to wrap with. For this make, we have chosen gold as it compliments our green crystal beautifully. As we continue onto other shapes and colours of crystals, you will notice that we use silver wire. The most important thing to remember when choosing your materials is the gauge of your wire! It needs to be very soft, thin, and easy to manipulate - giving it the ability to bend in the way you would like for your creation.

BUYING YOUR WIRE:

When buying wire to wrap, it's best to purchase craft wire as this has been specifically chosen to be used for this technique. Otherwise, we would say 0.2mm - 0.5mm wire is perfect. It's a very soft, easy to bend wire with the tendencies to be used for intricate wirework.

Top Tips – Be careful when buying 'plated' wire. It is sometimes less practical because the plating can wear off when bending and shaping!

EXTRA EQUIPMENT:

Once you start to feel confident with wire wrapping, you can begin introducing some other tools into your work to make your wire wrapping experience a little bit easier. Round nose pliers will be your best friend! By using round nose pliers, you can create very easy loops with your wire (which you will see later). They also help the wire to bend inwards at the end of your make to avoid any sharp and spikey finishes.

Don't worry if you don't have pliers. You can achieve the same outcome by using the circumference of an old pencil to help you.

ADDED EXTRAS!

You can literally wrap anything with wire wrapping, so why stop at crystals? Below are some alternative, stones you can use to make more beautiful jewellery and show off your skills!

SEA GLASS

Sea glass is a naturally weathered element which is found washed up on our beaches after many years of tumbling in the ocean. What was once a broken piece of a medicine bottle from the 1950's, can now be your new piece of recycled jewellery. How cool is that?!

CERAMIC

Ceramic is a fantastic material to wrap in wire due to its natural flat surface and rough edges. Like sea glass, there are many little pieces of ceramic washed up on our coastlines daily. Why not pick some up, give it a clean and upcycle into a new pair of earrings?

WARNINGS!

All the makes included in this book are designed specifically for adults.

When working with pliers, wire cutters and wire ensure you keep them in a safe place e.g. box in your workplace. Keep all tools and equipment in a safe, locked place when not working.

Keep the sharp end of the pliers away from you and your eyes at all times.

Keep all contents and tools and finished products out of the reach of children.

MAKE WITH KIT CONTENTS!

CRYSTAL PENDANT

CRYSTAL PENDANT

Great gift idea- make something special for a loved one or friend, or treat yourself to something special.

YOU WILL NEED
- Round Nose Pliers
- Flat nose Pliers
- Pencil
- Wire Cutters

KIT INCLUDES
- 1x Large Crystal
- 2x Crystal
- Gold coloured wire
- 1x Gold coloured chain with clasps
- 1x Pair of earring hooks

METHOD

Crystal Pendant on Gold Chain

1. Take your piece of wire and cut it into three 20cm pieces. Take one piece of the wire and bend it in half so that the two ends meet. Find the middle part of that wire and place your pliers (or a pencil) in the middle to create a gentle loop.

2. Holding your wire tightly, in one hand and your pliers in the other, start to twist your wire around your round nose pliers until your twisted wire measures around 3cm.

3. Gently remove your pliers and place your wire on the part of the crystal you would like it to sit. The twisted part of your wire will need a space of around 1cm above your crystal. Separating the two pieces of wire, gently fold these around the bottom part of your crystal and bring them around to the back (see second picture).

4. On the back of your crystal, fold the two wires over each other and then start to twist these together again like you did in step 2. Continue twisting until you get to the top of your crystal.

5. You now need to connect the front and the back part together. You guessed how you do this – twist!
Using the long piece of wire from the back of your crystal, bring this to the front and gently twist around the front stem just underneath where your loop is.

6. Once you have completed step 5 and all your wire has been wrapped, all that's left to do is attach your chain through the loop. Well done! You now have a wire wrapped crystal pendant!

Crystal Earrings with Gold Hooks

1. This is where we use the remaining two pieces of your wire to make your matching earrings! Start off by making sure you have all the materials you are going to need for this make.

2. Take your first piece of wire and like you did for the pendant – repeat the process of creating your loop with the round nose pliers. Twist your wire but this time, only 1.5cm down.

3. Place your wire on the crystal, leaving a space of around 0.5cm at the top. This time it doesn't have to be as long because we are making earrings - we don't want them to hang too much! As before, slowly bend the wire down to the base of your crystal.

4. Once you have reached the bottom of your crystal, slowly bring the two wires around to the back and cross them over halfway up your crystal. Start to twist the remaining wire together.

5. Once your two ends meet at the top, begin twisting these together. Bring them in as one and until your crystal is securely held in place.

6. Using a pair of flat nose pliers, gently open the loop on the hook fastening. Thread on your circular loop. Once attached, use your pliers to close the gap back up. Repeat the process to create your second earring.

NOTES

Use the space below to make your own personal notes on the previous project to help when you come back to make it again!

HORIZONTAL WRAP

HORIZONTAL WRAP

A unique way to wrap your crystal, glass or ceramic for amazing bespoke jewellery.

YOU WILL NEED
- Round nose pliers
- Flat nose pliers
- Pencil
- Wire cutters
- 1x Crystal
- Silver wire
- 1 x Silver chain with clasps

METHOD

1. Start by cutting a piece of wire 40cm in length. For this piece, we are going to wrap A LOT - make sure you have a little bit extra! Wrap the end of your wire around the circumference of the pencil 4-5 times.

2. Remove your wire from the pencil. Now, tuck in the little bit from the end of your wire which could be sticking out.

3. Take the crystal you have chosen. Holding the end of the wire against one side of the crystal, gently push the wire and bend around to the other side. Make sure the loop stays elevated above the crystal throughout this.

4. Now your wire is wrapped around the full length of your crystal, stop about a third of the way up and bend your wire to a right angle. Bring it around to the front again and complete a full circle around the middle of your crystal. This is your first wrap.

5. Keep wrapping your wire around your crystal, making your way up the whole of the crystal. Keep the wires very close to each other for extra effect. When you are getting near to the top and happy with your wrap, cut off the excess wire.

6. Once your excess wire has been cut off, tuck the loose ends into the rest of your wire wrap to avoid any sharp finishes. You are now ready to lace your pendant onto your necklace chain!

NOTES

Use the space below to make your own personal notes on the previous project to help when you come back to make it again!

CRISS CROSS WRAP

CRISS CROSS WRAP

Another unique way to wrap your jewellery for an added effect.

YOU WILL NEED
- Round nose pliers
- Flat nose pliers
- Pencil
- Wire cutters
- 1x Crystal
- Silver wire
- 1x Silver chain with clasps

METHOD

1. For this next make, we're going to keep it nice and simple. All you will need is a 30 cm cut piece of wire, a pencil, and a 5cm crystal.

2. Find the middle part of your wire and loop it around the middle of a pencil. Use the two loose ends of wire and tightly twist round each other until you have around 3cm of twisted wire. Slip your loop off the pencil.

3. Lay your wire flat on your surface (with the loop facing up) and position your crystal right in the middle of this. Holding both lengths of wire together, start in one corner and go to the other, gently wrapping in whichever way you want to go, but keeping those two wires held together.

4. After you have gone from corner to corner and up to down, try to look and see if there is any unsecure area. Wrap your two wires there. This is your design - you can literally take the wire in whichever direction you would like!

5. Once you're happy with how your pendant looks and you are confident that your crystal is secure, use your wire cutters to cut down the excess wire.

6. Gently twist the small loose ends up the stem of your hook until they are no longer poking out. Now it's time to attach your chain!

NOTES

Use the space below to make your own personal notes on the previous project to help when you come back to make it again!

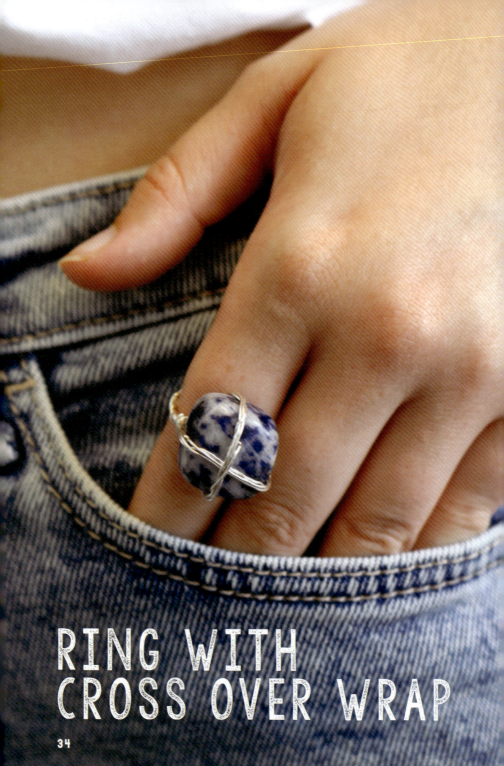

RING WITH CROSS OVER WRAP

RING WITH CROSS OVER WRAP

Make your ring stand out with this wire wrapping technique or create your own design.

YOU WILL NEED

- Round nose pliers
- Flat nose pliers
- Pencil
- Wire cutters
- 1 x Crystal
- Silver wire
- Mandrel/ Small tube

METHOD

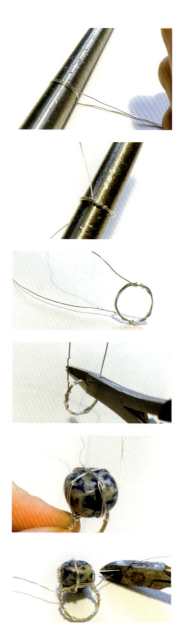

1. Firstly, grab your wire (60cm), crystal and if you have one – a ring mandrel. This is an essential as this is how you will determine the size and shape of your ring. If you do not have a mandrel, you could use something similar in width to a ring e.g. a lipstick.

2. Stretch your wire out and find the middle. Wrap this part around the mandrel, crossing the wires over, wrap again. Continue this until you have wrapped your wire around the mandrel three times.

3. Use the loose ends of wire to intertwine around the ring you have formed. This will solidify your ring shape. Once you have done this 3-4 times each side, remove from the mandrel.

4. Using a pair of flat nose pliers, flatten the edge of where you want your stone to sit. You need this part to sit flat so that your crystal can sit comfortably and won't move around.

5. Pull the two side pieces up around your crystal and bend over the top and back down again. Make sure you take the wire underneath the middle part of your ring to secure it each time. When looping back through, cross over the opposite way. Repeat this process 3-4 times.

6. When you are happy that your crystal is securely in place, grab your wire cutters and trim down the excess wire. Use your flat nose pliers to tuck the little bits of excess wire underneath the bottom of your crystal.

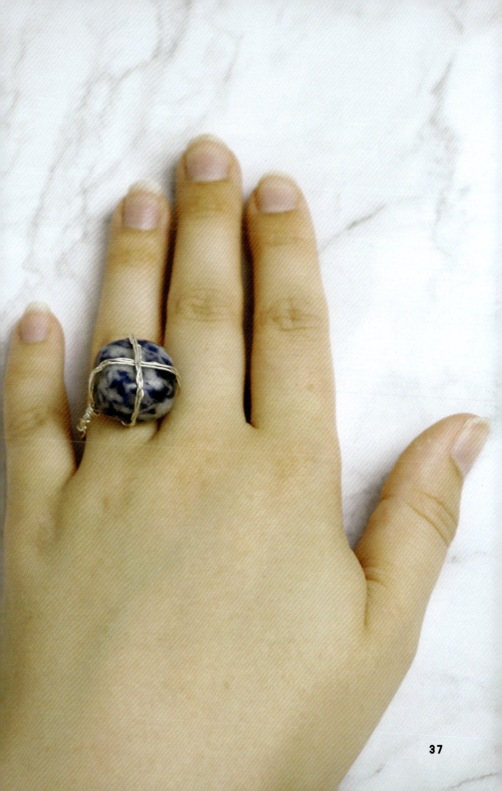

NOTES

Use the space below to make your own personal notes on the previous project to help when you come back to make it again!

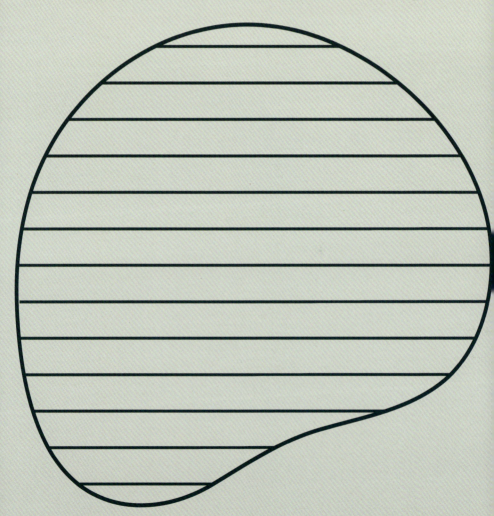

LOOP WRAP

LOOP WRAP

Another great way to wrap your jewellery for an eye catching piece!

YOU WILL NEED

- Round nose Pliers
- Flat nose pliers
- Pencil
- Wire cutters
- 1 x Crystal
- Silver wire
- Mandrel/ Small tube

METHOD

1. Cut a piece of wire 40cm in length and find the middle section of that wire. As we have done before, wrap the middle part around your round nose pliers.

2. Holding the pliers tightly in one hand and your wire in the other, twist the two wires around one another until you have around 6-7cm of twisted wire. Then, gently bend the wire over the top of your crystal, leaving adequate room above. This will be your hook.

3. Holding the top part tightly in place, keep twisting your wires until you have twisted all the way to the bottom of your crystal.

4. When you are at the bottom, separate your two wires out so they face in different directions.

5. Now, bend these two wires upwards, keeping hold of your crystal very tightly so the rest of it doesn't move. Bring them up enough so they can thread through the original loop you created for the front of the pendant.

6. Once you have looped the wires through the hole, bring them upwards and around to the back. Twist to tighten in place and cut off the excess wire with your wire cutters. Loop your chain through the twisted hook at the top. Well done!

NOTES

Use the space below to make your own personal notes on the previous project to help when you come back to make it again!